JRR Tolkien

His life, work and faith

by
Raymond Edwards

All booklets are published thanks to the
generous support of the members of the
Catholic Truth Society

CATHOLIC TRUTH SOCIETY

PUBLISHERS TO THE HOLY SEE

All rights reserved. First published 2012 by The Incorporated Catholic Truth Society, 40-46 Harleyford Road London SE11 5AY Tel: 020 7640 0042 Fax: 020 7640 0046. This edition © 2012 The Incorporated Catholic Truth Society.

ISBN 978 1 86082 827 0

Front cover images: *John Ronald Reuel Tolkien with a pipe* © Mondadori/ GettyImages. *Mount Cook, Mount Cook National Park, Canterbury, New Zealand* © Colin Monteath/ Hedgehog House/ Minden Pictures/ Corbis.

Contents

"Out of the darkness of my life, so much frustrated, I put before you the one great thing to love on earth: the Blessed Sacrament... There you will find romance, glory, honour, fidelity, and the true way of all your loves on earth, and more than that: Death: by the divine paradox, that which ends life, and demands the surrender of all, and yet by the taste - or foretaste - of which alone can what you seek in your earthly relationships (love, faithfulness, joy) be maintained, or take on that complexion of reality, of eternal endurance, which every man's heart desires."

"The only cure for sagging or fainting faith is Communion. Though always Itself, perfect and complete and inviolate, the Blessed Sacrament does not operate completely and once for all in any of us. Like the act of Faith it must be continuous and grow by exercise. Frequency is of the highest effect. Seven times a week is more nourishing than seven times at intervals."

The Letters of JRR Tolkien, pp. 53-54, 338-339.

Introduction

It is late in the year; under the vast domed Great Hall of the new University of Birmingham, rows of temporary beds are set up, filled with sick men, most newly back from France. One of them is writing in a small school exercise book.

The year is 1916, and he has been some months with his battalion on the Somme. Already many of his school and university friends have been killed. Compared with them, he is lucky; he has been struck down with a debilitating persistent fever, spread through the trenches by the ubiquitous lice. He is getting better, now, although still weak and exhausted and unfit to return to his unit. Soon, he will be discharged, and able to go to a Staffordshire village to stay with the wife he had married only eight months ago, two months before he was sent to France. Meanwhile, he is writing: stories of an age of myth, of elves and dragons and love and despair and hope lost and renewed. His name is Ronald Tolkien.

The stories he wrote at this time were not published for another seventy years; but the themes and characters he described in them gradually found shape and led directly to his famous books, *The Hobbit* and *The Lord of the Rings*. Here, whilst first recovering in hospital, then on a series of home service postings, began his life's work: a corpus of imaginative writing whose overmastering theme, he declared late in life, was Death.

Tolkien is now best-known as an author - his published writings run to twenty or so thick volumes - but he was many other things beside: husband, father to four children, professor of ancient language at Oxford, devout Catholic. How did he combine all of these things? How did his writing connect with the rest of his life, and his work? What sort of man was he, who arguably changed forever the sort of books that are written, and read? It is probably impossible to answer all of these questions, especially in a booklet of this size; but I hope to give hints about some possible answers, and some helpful places to look.

Many readers of his books, and even more those who have seen the film adaptations, may not realise that Tolkien was not just a practising Catholic, but one whose faith was utterly central to his writing. I will look, briefly, at some of the ways this is true.

Some converts to Catholicism have said that reading *The Lord of the Rings* helped to 'baptise' their imagination, or prepare their souls for the gift of faith, despite the absence of any explicit reference to Christianity in the work. As we shall see, Tolkien himself admitted that it was "a fundamentally religious and Catholic work"; at times he seems to have felt divine providence had a hand in the writing.

I have assumed that anyone reading this booklet is likely to have read, or at least seen the film versions of, *The Lord of the Rings* and *The Hobbit*. Accordingly I presume some knowledge of what happens in the books, and have not given extensive discussions of them. There are plenty of good books that do this; some are listed in the section on Further Reading.

The Making of a Philologist

"I'm a philologist," said Lowdham,
"which means a misunderstood man." [1]

Family

It may surprise some to learn that Tolkien, in many ways a quintessentially English writer, was born in South Africa.

Despite his surname, the German in his background was minimal;[2] the Tolkiens were solid Birmingham middle-class, whilst his mother's family, the Suffields, were originally Worcestershire farming stock. His grandfather, John Tolkien, had been a piano maker; his business failed, and he turned to selling music. He had four children; his wife died, and he then remarried. Tolkien's father, Arthur, was the eldest child of this second marriage. Arthur had been working for Lloyds Bank in Birmingham for some years when, in 1888, aged thirty-one, he met Mabel Suffield and they became engaged. She was only eighteen, however, and her father (once a prosperous draper, now, after his business had failed, a commercial traveller for Jeyes Fluid) forbade her to marry for two years. The following year, Arthur Tolkien sailed for South Africa, where he had got a job with the Bank of Africa in Cape

Colony; the next year, he was made manager of their branch in Bloemfontein, capital of the Orange Free State. He had significantly more responsibility, and better pay, than he could have hoped for at home. This made marriage possible; in March 1891, Mabel, who was now twenty-one, took ship for South Africa. On 16th April, she and Arthur were married in the Anglican Cathedral in Cape Town. They lived in Bloemfontein, in a house attached to the bank where Arthur was manager.

There, on 3rd January 1892, their first child was born. He was christened John Ronald Reuel. Two years later, his brother Hilary was born.

Arthur Tolkien enjoyed the African climate; his wife did not, and was moreover concerned that Ronald was suffering from the constant heat. In April 1895, accordingly, she took both boys home to England for an extended leave. Arthur stayed in South Africa; he could not afford to leave his job for any amount of time, but hoped to come and join them before long. That November, he fell ill with rheumatic fever, and could not face the rigours of a voyage and the English winter. Mabel and the boys spent Christmas with her family. In January, after a short recovery, Arthur fell ill again; Mabel decided she must return to South Africa to look after him. Before she could make arrangements, however, Arthur suddenly deteriorated. On 14th February 1896, Mabel received a telegram saying he had had a haemorrhage and she should expect the worst; the next day, he died. Arthur Tolkien was only thirty-nine. Mabel Tolkien was twenty-six; her sons, four and two.

Thereafter his mother brought up Ronald and his brother alone. They lodged in a semi-detached cottage in the small village of Sarehole, then a mile or so outside Birmingham. It is now a suburb of the city, but in 1896 was a real country village with a watermill, a river, and strong thickets of trees.

Mabel had always been an active churchgoer; she became involved, now, in a 'high' Anglo-Catholic parish. This led her to Catholicism; in 1900, along with her sister, she became a Catholic, and was summarily disinherited by her family.[3]

Orphaned and educated

Mabel was an intelligent and highly literate woman; rather than send her boys to school, she taught them herself. This also helped her financially; she had only a small income from some shares left by Arthur. As well as conventional subjects, she taught them botany and drawing (both of which were interests that stayed with Ronald throughout his life), and gave them a grounding in languages: French, German and Latin. From the first, it was clear that Ronald had a strong talent in this area.

In 1900, Ronald was sent to his father's old school, King Edward's School in Birmingham, an ancient grammar school, and probably the best in the area. The fees were paid by a Tolkien uncle. Mabel moved the household from rural Sarehole to a rented house in Moseley in the city centre, near a Catholic church. Ronald was desolate at the move, and was at first unhappy at school, but after a term settled in well enough. After two years, Mabel moved them again, this time to be closer to the Birmingham Oratory, as she had grown to dislike the church they had been attending. One of the Fathers of the Oratory, Fr Francis Xavier Morgan, half Welsh, half Anglo-Spanish (his family were in the wine trade), became a family friend and (we would probably say today) spiritual director to Mabel.

The Oratory also ran a school, St Philip's. Ronald and Hilary were enrolled there in 1902, but after a year, it became clear that although the education was Catholic and the fees were lower than King Edward's, the schooling was not of the same quality; and Ronald needed to be stretched. His mother took the boys out of school and taught them at home again. With the help of coaching from his mother, and from his aunt Jane (who was a maths teacher), he won a scholarship to King Edward's, and returned there in 1903.

At the start of 1904, both boys were ill. Mabel was exhausted with nursing them, and in April was admitted to hospital. She was diagnosed with diabetes. This was before the discovery of insulin, and there was no effective treatment except rest. Ronald and Hilary were sent to stay with relatives; by June, however, Mabel had recovered enough to leave hospital. Fr Francis Morgan arranged for her and the boys to stay in a cottage near the Oratory retreat house at Rednal, in the Worcestershire countryside.

They stayed at Rednal for the summer and autumn; it was a welcome return to the country, although when school began Ronald had to walk a mile to catch a train into Birmingham.

At the start of November, after five months of country life, Mabel's illness suddenly and catastrophically returned. She fell into a diabetic coma; six days later, on November 14th 1904, aged only thirty-four, Mabel Tolkien died.

It is probably fair to say Ronald Tolkien never got over his mother's death. His first biographer noted that, thereafter, his naturally cheerful and outgoing manner was counterbalanced by periods of intense despondency, when he felt "a deep sense of impending loss. Nothing was safe. Nothing would last. No battle would be won for ever."[4] The interests she had given him - botany, drawing, the English countryside, language - were now charged with a strong memory of her; so, too, was the Catholic religion.

Her boys, thirteen and eleven, became wards of Fr Francis Morgan. Some of their Tolkien and Suffield relatives wanted to contest Mabel's will, and raise the boys Protestant; Fr Francis arranged for them to live with the one Suffield aunt who was content for them to stay Catholic. He ensured that both brothers' education continued (at King Edward's). He also supplemented the Tolkiens' meagre patrimony from his own private income, and continued to do so for some years. Many years later, Tolkien said his example outweighed that of all the disagreeable or even plain bad priests he had met.

School now assumed a large part in Tolkien's life. Greek and Latin were the backbone of the curriculum, but he was also taught a good deal of English literature, including Chaucer in the original. He was academically strong, and was soon placed regularly at the top of his class. He was also, although slightly built, a keen rugby player.

His first close friend at school was Christopher Wiseman, son of a Methodist minister; later, when Wiseman senior was appointed President of the Wesleyan Methodist Conference, Fr Francis Morgan referred to him as 'the Pope of Wesley'. Tolkien and Wiseman were academic rivals as well as friends, and both played rugby energetically and well; they took to calling themselves 'the Great Twin Brethren.' Wiseman was a mathematician, and an amateur musician and composer.

Tolkien began dabbling in what was to become an abiding interest: making up his own languages. As a boy, he and two of his cousins had, like many children, made up a code language; now, armed with a formidable battery of actual languages (as well as Latin, Greek, French (which he disliked) and German, he also had some Spanish (via Fr Francis), some Welsh, some Old Norse and, thanks to a schoolmaster, Old and Middle English), he began to devise a properly structured language, somewhat after the phonetic model of Spanish, that he called Naffarin. Later, a schoolfellow who had bought, by mistake, *A Primer of the Gothic Language* (by an Oxford professor named Joseph Wright), passed this on to Tolkien. Gothic is the most ancient Germanic language still preserved; Tolkien was bowled over by it.

It was the custom for the school library to be run by some of the senior boys; Tolkien and Wiseman were two of them. They made two particular friends amongst their fellow Librarians: Rob Gilson (son of the school's headmaster), and Geoffrey Bache Smith. Gilson had a flair for drawing and design, Smith was a talented poet.

The four of them together referred to themselves, humorously, as the 'TCBS', which stood for 'Tea Club [and] Barrovian Society' after their habit of meeting for tea and conversation, both (illicitly) in the school library, and at Barrow's Stores in the city. This abbreviation, which began as a slightly arch joke, became convenient shorthand for their collective sense of themselves, and their artistic ambitions. It is easy to exaggerate the importance of this type of schoolboy connection, or from the comfortable disillusion of middle age, perhaps, to mock the vaunting idealism of teenage boys; but the fact remains that it was this time, and these friends, which helped Tolkien to discover that he wanted, above all, to write; and to write, in particular, something characteristically English in the way that, say, Greek or Norse myth was characteristic of those languages or cultures, something England had once had but because of historical accident had lost. Tolkien gradually determined to do this as a poet. As much as anything, though, Tolkien was excited by language - by the forms of words, in addition to (and to an extent separable from) their meaning. In each language he knew, he found a unique element of aesthetic pleasure that, somehow, chimed with his own innate preferences. Years later, he proposed the theory that we each of us have a 'native language' which satisfies all our particular linguistic predilections, and that this language is not our 'first-learned language' or mother-tongue. Much of Tolkien's life can be seen, from one angle, as a search for this 'native language'.

First Love

At the start of 1908, Tolkien, now sixteen, and his brother Hilary moved from their aunt's house to live as lodgers with the Faulkners, a wine merchant and his wife, in Edgbaston; they had as a fellow lodger a nineteen year-old girl, Edith Bratt. She and Tolkien became friends, and allies against Mrs Faulkner's constricting household regime. By the following summer, they decided they were in love. They began to meet in secret.

Like Tolkien, Edith was an orphan; her mother had died when she was fourteen. Unlike him, she was illegitimate;

her mother had been a governess in her father's house, and Edith had never been recognised as his daughter by him or his family. She was musical, playing the piano well, and was by background an Anglican.

Whether this youthful romance would have, under other circumstances, amounted to anything is obviously unknowable and probably irrelevant; as it was, Tolkien's guardian, Father Francis Morgan, learned of the connection in the autumn of 1909, and, seeing only something to distract Tolkien from his schoolwork (he was supposed to be studying hard for an Oxford scholarship) insisted it stop. Soon afterwards, Tolkien sat and failed the scholarship exam. Without financial help from an award, he had no chance of attending the University. In the new year, Fr Francis arranged for Tolkien and his brother to move to different lodgings.

1910 started darkly for Tolkien; his academic future, and his happiness with Edith, both seemed imperilled. Throughout his life, Tolkien was subject to black moods, gloom, periodic feelings of hopelessness. Outwardly, he kept busy and sociable, but in his private diary he was often near despair.

Tolkien saw Edith again, secretly; Fr Francis found out. He formally forbade Tolkien to see her until he should come of age on his twenty-first birthday three years later. Edith, meanwhile, had arranged to move to Cheltenham, to live with family friends.

This business, forbidding an eighteen-year old young man to see a girl, may seem to cast Fr Francis Morgan in a tyrannical light. We need to see this within the context of its time: long engagements, and marriages postponed for financial reasons or because of reservations on the part of one or the other family, were a normal part of Victorian life, and were not unusual in the Edwardian age; Francis Morgan may have been a touch old-fashioned, but no one would have supposed him wrong, or necessarily unreasonable, to act in this way, and indeed he might have seemed irresponsible had he not done so. Tolkien was still legally a minor, and had only a very modest income from his father's estate; he could not possibly afford to get married without a good job and that, for him, meant getting a degree. His academic gifts were obvious, and Fr Francis was anxious to help him make the most of them. Tolkien could not in any case have got married or engaged without his guardian's permission.

Tolkien's acquiescence in this, which may seem odd to us, can be partly explained by the social expectations of the time; for the rest, we should look to Tolkien's attitude to his religion. He was convinced, not unreasonably, that his mother's conversion and in particular her family's reaction to it had contributed to her early death: better medical care, which they could have enabled, might well have brought her through the crisis that caused her death. This made her, in some fashion, 'a martyr for the faith'. Fr Francis Morgan's subsequent role as guardian was by no means a perfunctory one. He was almost the exact age Tolkien's own father would have been; aside from considerable financial generosity, he also took a close interest in the Tolkien brothers. They usually came to the Oratory to serve his early Mass, and have breakfast in the refectory before going to school; Tolkien said later he had been "virtually a junior inmate of the Oratory house, which contained many learned fathers (largely 'converts')."[5] Francis Morgan, he said, had been his "second father."

Whilst he may have been sometimes privately miserable, Tolkien still had the energy and enthusiasm of early youth. He immersed himself in work, both in preparation for another Oxford scholarship exam, and for his own private ends. He had by now a good knowledge of Gothic and Old English and could discourse at length on comparative philology; invited to talk on this subject to the sixth form, Tolkien, with the confidence of his age, gave three hours of lecture and would have said more, had the master not stopped him. The school had the custom of holding debates in Latin; this, for Tolkien, was all too easy, and he once, in the role of Greek ambassador to the Senate, spoke wholly in Greek; on other occasions, in the character of barbarian envoys, he broke into Gothic or Old English. Tolkien's hobby of 'private languages' developed, too; he devised hypothetical Gothic words to supplement the meagre vocabulary that had survived from the historical language, and further elaborated his 'Naffarin' language.

Perhaps not all of this was strictly pertinent to an Oxford scholarship; but it reveals him as a young man of varied and exuberant intellectual interests. He also kept up his involvement in rugby and theatricals.

In December 1910, he was awarded an Exhibition (a minor scholarship) worth £60 a year to Exeter College, Oxford, to read Litterae Humaniores (Classics). Added to this was a leaving bursary from King Edward's, and some money from Fr Francis. Tolkien would not be rich, but he could now go to Oxford.

University and Edith

In October 1911, Tolkien matriculated at the University.

Edith, meanwhile, had made a life for herself in Cheltenham. The family friends she lived with, the Jessops, had a large house and a comfortable life. Edith was socially active, in particular in the local Anglican church. She had always been an accomplished pianist, and now took great pleasure playing the organ at her parish. During this time she injured her back whilst playing the organ; she never fully recovered.

At midnight on 3rd January 1913, Tolkien turned twenty-one. He at once sat down and wrote to Edith, asking her when they might be reunited. She told him by return that she had got engaged to the brother of a school friend;

she had lost hope that Tolkien would still love her. As soon as he could, Tolkien went to Cheltenham to see her; on 8th January, she broke off her engagement and agreed to marry him instead. Her family were unhappy at Tolkien's apparent lack of prospects, and more so at his Catholicism, particularly as he insisted that a reluctant Edith should herself convert. She resisted, but Tolkien was insistent and she gave in. When she told the Jessops she meant to become a Catholic, she was told to find somewhere else to live. In June, together with an older cousin, she moved to Warwick and found lodgings there.

After a short and not wholly satisfactory course of instruction from the Catholic priest in Warwick, Edith was received into the Church on 8th January 1914, the first anniversary of her reunion with Tolkien.

Tolkien, meanwhile, was finding his time at Oxford agreeable (he threw himself into college social life), but the work frankly dull. He had trouble maintaining interest in Greek dramas he had read at school, and already knew as well as he cared to. He was easily distracted onto intellectual (mostly linguistic) bypaths. The one exception to this was the optional paper he took in Comparative Philology. For this he was taught by the remarkable Joseph Wright, author of the Gothic Primer he had owned since he was a schoolboy. Wright had been a mill-hand, who taught himself to read aged fifteen, then at night-school learnt Latin, French and German; aged twenty-one, he walked to Heidelberg to spend his savings on a term's study at the university. Once there, he stayed and took a doctorate in philology. He returned to England in 1888 and moved to Oxford. In 1891, aged thirty-six, he was appointed deputy to Max Müller, Professor of Comparative Philology; two years later he succeeded to the Chair.

Philology

It is unlikely that anyone at a British university today will have heard of philology, let alone studied it, under that name at least. During the late nineteenth century, however, it was one of the most exciting and innovative areas of scholarship. Starting from observed similarities between languages (even some widely separated by time and distance, like Sanskrit and Latin), scholars had discovered clear and definite rules governing how languages have evolved and how they are related. This allowed them to make reliable inferences about other languages, ancestral to those we know, that have not survived: such as 'proto-Germanic', ancestor of English, German and the Scandinavian languages, or, further back, 'Indo-European', the great progenitor of a vast family of languages stretching from Europe to India. Philology, the study of language under this aspect, could now give us the very words our distant ancestors had spoken before recorded history. Looking at the words they used told us, also, something about what their lives had been like, and maybe even where they had lived. The late years of the nineteenth century saw a profusion of books and articles describing the culture and beliefs of the speakers of the languages scholarship had recovered. Some of these early studies seem, now, fanciful or unrealistic; but the attempt itself remains both valuable and fascinating. Tolkien began to apply exactly this technique to his own invented languages; the search for a context for them was at the heart of his maturing imagined world.

All of this was in the background of Tolkien's mind in these years, and lay behind the teaching of Joseph Wright; but we should not think that Tolkien was wholly studious; in fact, he was for his first four terms at Oxford if anything rather slack. He read widely, but much of what he read was unrelated to his prescribed course of study. Notably, he found a Finnish grammar in his college library, and was immediately intoxicated by the language; he described the experience as like discovering a hidden cellar full of "amazing wine of a kind and flavour never tasted before." He abandoned work on Naffarin, and began to devise a 'private language' based on Finnish. Not that all his distractions were scholarly; he was highly sociable, and took a full and lively part in the various concerts, drinks parties, dining clubs and literary societies at his college. He was also less diligent than before about the practice of his religion. He was both living slightly beyond his means and, apart from philology, doing little more work than was absolutely required.

In February 1913, after four terms of this agreeable and educative slackness, and a month after the excitements of his reunion with Edith, Tolkien sat his first public examination, Honour Moderations, and was placed in the second class. This was not disastrous, but as an Exhibitioner of the college he was expected to do better. His tutors, fortunately, were not fools; they noted he had obtained a pure alpha in his Comparative Philology paper (a combination of natural aptitude and the teaching of Joseph Wright), and suggested he transfer to the English School the following term. The College authorities generously allowed him to transfer his Exhibition, which was strictly for the study of classics, to this new school.

Tolkien's tutor was to be Kenneth Sisam, a New Zealander only four years his senior who had already established a formidable reputation as an Anglo-Saxon philologist and who was, besides, a collaborator and protégé of the great liturgical scholar Edmund Bishop.

A Mythology for England

On 4th August 1914, Britain entered the First World War; many of Tolkien's friends and contemporaries joined up to fight. He did not, but planned to complete the last year of his degree. This was not from a lack of patriotic feeling, or objection to the war or its aims, although Tolkien refused to join in the widespread vilifying of German culture, which he revered as the fountain-head of philology and as bearer of the Northern spirit. But Tolkien was a poor man, engaged to be married, and without any obvious 'prospects' except what his mind and learning could bring him. For him, his future required getting a good degree; and so he planned to return to Oxford in October. The war could wait.

In the meantime, he went to stay with his aunt, Jane Neave, at her farm at Gedling in Nottinghamshire. On 24th September 1914, he wrote a poem called, *The Voyage of Éarendel the Evening Star*. This was the first real text of what was to become his life's work, the elaboration of a world-mythology in which his invented languages could be at home. For ease of reference, I will refer to this whole body of writing as Tolkien's legendarium.[6]

Amongst the Old English poems Tolkien read at Oxford was *Crist*, a ragbag collection of religious verse, much of it dull stuff. Its first section is a series of 'Advent lyrics', based around the 'O Antiphons' of that season. Amongst them, glossing the antiphon *O Oriens* ('O Rising Sun, you are the splendour of eternal life and the sun of justice. O come and enlighten those who live in darkness and in the shadow of death'), is this couplet:

> *Éalá Éarendel engla beorhtast*
> *ofer middangeard monnum sended.*
> 'Hail, Éarendel, brightest of angels
> over middle-earth sent to men.'

The word or name *éarendel* intrigued Tolkien. According to the glossaries, it was a star or planet, perhaps Venus the morning star, or Rigel in Orion; here, it may refer to John the Baptist as a forerunner of Christ, the Sun of Justice. But it was the form of the word that fascinated Tolkien: it was, he thought, both like other Old English words and yet, somehow, of a different and nobler style. In his poem, he tried to explore what the word might have actually meant: it is the name of a mariner who pilots his ship across the sky from the west to the light of dawn, hearing the joys and sorrows of the men of earth betweentimes. It is an early work, but in its way remarkable for what it tries to do.

One of Tolkien's great laments was the absence of any specifically English body of myth and legend, comparable to that collected and synthesized for Germany by Jacob Grimm.[7] First the Norman Conquest, then early industrialisation had destroyed beyond recovery all but unmeaning fragments of the great body of legend and heroic story once native to England. What Tolkien was doing here, and what he continued to do throughout his life as a writer, was a form of philological enquiry: he examined the surviving evidence (for lost English legends, or lost or 'invented' languages) and tried to reconstruct what might have lain behind them: the story of Eärendil as it eventually developed (the great mariner who carries a Silmaril into the uttermost west, to plead for exiled men and elves in their dark oppression, and who is translated to the heavens as a new star, a sign of hope) Tolkien thought best explained the name *éarendel* as it appeared in Old English, and in some few other old northern contexts.

On 12th December 1914, the four TCBS friends met for a reunion, which they dubbed 'The Council of London'; their talk, that day, was of fundamentals: truth, religion, love, art, patriotic duty. Again, we may dismiss this as youthful idealism, but it seems to have unsealed in Tolkien a source of inspiration. Over the next few months, he wrote numerous poems, and elaborated his new neo-Finnish language, now called Qenya. He also continued training with the University Officers' Training Corps.

We have seen the approach Tolkien took to what he reckoned were the surviving linguistic fragments of Old English legend; he applied precisely this same method to the words of his 'private languages'. According to strict philology, their words also implied a world in which to place them, and to a great extent described it. Tolkien always insisted that this was the correct order of his inspiration: first language, then story. During the next two years, he wrote a number of poems whose core was some element of his private languages; the poems were an attempt to express something of this linguistic inspiration in a discursive way: to give the same effect in verse as he had received in a word or phrase of his 'Qenya'.

In June 1915, Tolkien took Final Schools; he was placed in the First Class. He had now done all he could to begin an academic career, and was free to join the army. He was commissioned into the Lancashire Fusiliers, which was GB Smith's regiment.[8] He hoped to join the same battalion as Smith; in the event, he was posted to another unit. He spent the next few months in Bedford and Staffordshire training with his unit; he also wrote and revised poems, and occasionally saw Edith, who was still living in Warwick.

On 22nd March 1916, Tolkien and Edith were married. A week later he received a publisher's letter rejecting a volume of his poems, titled *The Trumpets of Faerie*.

War

On 6th June 1916, Tolkien was ordered to France to join his battalion, the 11th Lancashire Fusiliers, in preparation for the Somme offensive. He had trained as a signals officer, which allowed him in some small way to use his aptitude for code and language.

On 1st July, the Battle of the Somme began. British attacks on this first day suffered severe losses; sixty thousand men were casualties, including almost twenty thousand dead. Amongst them was Rob Gilson, killed at the head of his men in no-man's-land. Tolkien and most of his battalion were in reserve during the first two weeks' fighting. On 15th and 16th July, they were sent into action. As a signals officer, Tolkien's job was less dangerous than, say, leading a platoon into action; but it was by no means a safe post. Casualties amongst all front line troops were high, and Tolkien was undoubtedly in danger. For the remainder of July and all of August, his battalion was rotated in and out of the front line. Periods of front-line duty were occupied mainly with digging and reinforcing trenches, rather than direct assaults across no-man's-land; but they were not without danger, and the battalion lost a steady trickle of men to shellfire and snipers. September was spent behind the lines, in training; then after a few more weeks in the front line, they took part, on 21st October, in a successful assault on the German trenches. The battalion lost about one hundred and fifty men killed and wounded; Tolkien was unhurt. The next day, they moved behind the lines to recuperate.

Tolkien's brother Hilary had enlisted in the army at the outbreak of war. He was in France from 1915 to the end of the war, serving as a bugler - which meant, amongst other things, acting as a stretcher-bearer under fire. He was several times wounded, although not seriously; each time, the Army authorities sent a telegram to his designated next-of-kin, who was his sister-in-law, Edith. We can only speculate on how she felt.

On 25th October 1916, behind the lines in Beauval, Tolkien began to feel ill; two days later, he reported sick with a fever of 103. He had caught what the troops knew as 'trench fever', and their medical officers as PUO, or 'pyrexia of unknown origin'. After the war it was discovered to be transmitted by lice, endemic in the trenches. Its symptoms were high fever, headaches, leg pain and subsequent extreme weakness; when severe, it could leave a legacy of depression. Thousands of men fell sick with it during the war; for many, like Tolkien, it probably saved their lives.

Tolkien was sent to hospital in Le Touquet, but got no better, and on 8th November was put on a ship for England. On 9th November he was admitted to a temporary hospital set up at the Edgbaston campus of Birmingham University. By mid-December, he was well enough to be discharged from hospital, but too weak to return to duty. He travelled to Great Haywood in Warwickshire, where Edith was living with her cousin.

On 29th November 1916, behind the front line, GB Smith was wounded by shellfire; the wound was minor, but became infected. He died five days later, on 3rd December 1916. Tolkien realised, when he heard the news, that if the TCBS was to come to anything, he would have to try also to say what Gilson and Smith had wanted to, but now could not.

At this time, whilst recovering in hospital and in lodgings, he began writing the first stories from what he called his *Book of Lost Tales*, the first efforts at his 'mythology for England'. Edith copied out some of his early tales. This is the only recorded collaboration by her in his imaginative world; for many years afterwards, he shared it, if at all, only with a few male intimates. The first *Tale* to be written down was *The Fall of Gondolin*, recounting the destruction of an elven city by hordes of goblins and fire-demons equipped with diabolic mechanical siege weapons; although written in Morris-influenced archaic prose, the mark of the War is clear on it.

At the end of February 1917, Tolkien was moved to a convalescent hospital in Harrogate; then, in mid-April, to the Humber Garrison. He was recovering, but was still too weak to return to France. Here he continued to write his *Book of Lost Tales*, and also compiled a lexicon of a second 'private language' to add to his existing Qenya. This second creation was closer to Welsh, and was called Goldogrin or Gnomish. Thereafter, although their names and the supposed details of their interrelations changed often, these two 'elvish' languages were at the heart of Tolkien's inventions. They eventually emerged, much changed, as Quenya and Sindarin.

One day in May or June that year, in a hemlock grove near Roos in Yorkshire, Tolkien watched Edith dance. This gave rise to one of the longest and most heart-felt of Tolkien's *Tales*, the *Tale of Tinúviel*, which became the story of Beren and Lúthien: a mortal man, fled from war and defeat, sees the elven-fair maiden Lúthien dancing amidst the hemlock-umbels of a forest, and falls in love; together, they overcome, for a while, the darkness and sorrow of their time, and pass beyond even death together.

Their first son was born in November 1917, after a difficult labour. He was named John Francis, after Fr Francis Morgan.

In May 1918, Tolkien's former battalion, the 11th Lancashire Fusiliers, was wiped out on the Aisne during the great German spring offensive.

Tolkien survived the Great War, but was not unmarked by it. Famously, in the 1966 preface to *The Lord of the Rings*, he noted: "By 1918, all but one of my close friends were dead." There were other effects, too: all too clearly, the Somme underlies his evocation of the werelit horrors of the Dead Marshes, the mounds of blasted earth around the approaches of Mordor, its hurrying columns of cursing soldiery. But these are just the superficial links. On one level, the losses of war galvanised his talent, to complete the work his TCBS friends now could not. Tolkien himself sometimes recognised this; at other times, he wondered whether the War had not stifled his development as a writer: "I was pitched into it all, just when I was full of stuff to write, and of things to learn; and never picked it all up again."[9] But this was written in a dark day, when his great book was hardly begun, and might never be finished; and all these things are, besides, forever unknowable. Tolkien's writing is rooted, certainly, in his vast and intuitive scholarship, but also in an imaginative reaction by an acutely sensitive and educated Catholic to the staggering trauma of the Great War, a collective experience that still informs and qualifies our view of 'civilised' man. Running through his work is a profound and often heartbreaking meditation on the ruinous perversion of goodness and civilisation, on the coterminous arising of aching beauty and unblinking malevolence from the same God-given faculty of sub-creation. Above all, his theme (as he said in a late interview) was "death! - inevitable death," that sets a term to all human achievement, that mars and frustrates our plans, and casts to ruin all we strive to build and create; and yet which is not the last word.

The Armistice was signed on 11th November, 1918; the guns at last fell silent, and the threads of pre-War life might, in some fashion, be picked up again. Tolkien was given permission, although still formally a soldier, to move to Oxford. He now needed to try to resume his academic career, laid aside three years before.

The Young Scholar

Dictionary Work

Back in Oxford, with a wife and child to support, Tolkien needed a job. He was recruited by the Rawlinson and Bosworth Professor of Anglo-Saxon, William Craigie, to work on the *Oxford English Dictionary* (*OED*); Craigie was also one of the *Dictionary's* editors, although Tolkien actually reported not to Craigie but to his senior colleague Henry Bradley. The *Dictionary* had been started in conscious emulation of the Grimms' *Deutsche Wörterbuch*, and was (and probably remains) the single most prestigious philological project in English. Tolkien had fallen on his feet.

He began work in January 1919. In later years, Tolkien used to claim, half-seriously, that he had written the *OED*; in fact, he wrote initial entries, and very comprehensive etymologies, for several dozen words beginning W-, and advised on numerous others. For any one person to claim to have written this astonishing book was a joke obvious to anyone who knew even the smallest thing about it; but Tolkien's time at the *Dictionary* should not be dismissed. He himself claimed to have learned, in those two years, more philology than in any other comparable period of his life.

Tolkien's brother Hilary, meanwhile, after four years in the army, bought a fruit farm near Evesham in Worcestershire, and for the next half-century grew and sold plums.

Tolkien's pay at the *OED* was modest; he looked about for other work, which might help with finding a more permanent (and better paid) academic post.

In June 1919, his sometime tutor Kenneth Sisam, now ensconced at the University Press, realised he didn't have time to compile a glossary for an undergraduate anthology, *Fourteenth Century Verse and Prose*, he was preparing, and asked Tolkien to produce one for him. Tolkien set to work with a thoroughness that exceeded what Sisam had expected or required.

Work on the glossary took time; in June 1919, he laid aside, incomplete, the *Book of Lost Tales* he had been writing, on and off, since 1916. By this time it comprised fourteen tales in all; three of these (*Tinúviel*, *Turambar*, *The Fall of Gondolin*) were the 'Great Tales' which Tolkien planned to tell at greater length.

Tolkien also at this time found work as an 'extern tutor' for the university - someone, that is, who holds no formal position, but is employed to teach undergraduates a particular subject, usually one outside the competence of their main subject tutor. There were few who could teach English philology, and a growing number of undergraduates in the Oxford English School; many of them were at the women's colleges, and here Tolkien had the additional advantage of being married, which meant a woman student's college did not have to find an additional person to chaperone her during her tutorials with him. By the end of May 1920, he was getting enough regular work of this sort to be able to leave the *OED* and teach full time, giving classes as well as individual tutorials.

Early in 1920, Edith again became pregnant.

That June, Sisam told him there was a job coming up at the University of Leeds, as Reader in English Language. Tolkien applied, and was successful. The job began that October; it payed a round £600 a year. Their second son, Michael, was born in October 1920, soon before they moved north.

Leeds

Tolkien now started a busy and diligent time at Leeds, teaching a growing number of students specialising in English philology, and encouraging (with some success) the incorporation of philological elements (history of the language, and the reading of early texts) into the wider English course. His *Middle English Vocabulary* (which began as Sisam's glossary) came out in 1922, and was followed, three years later, by an edition of the Middle English poem *Sir Gawain and the Green Knight*, done jointly with a Leeds colleague, EV Gordon.

In 1922, Tolkien applied, unsuccessfully, for the Chair of English Literature at Leeds, after its previous incumbent, George Gordon, had been elected to one of the Oxford Merton chairs. The Leeds Vice-Chancellor privately assured Tolkien that a chair of English Language would be created for him. This was done in October 1924, when Tolkien became Professor of English Language.

He had not abandoned work on his legendarium, but rather than continuing or revising the *Lost Tales*, he began to retell some of them in verse. Tolkien still thought of himself as primarily a poet, or perhaps (like William Morris) someone who could work in prose and verse with equal facility.

His first effort, a *Lay of the Fall of Gondolin*, was in a (not very successful) hexameter line, and was early abandoned. He then decided to use the Old English alliterative line, the same verse form used in the great monuments of Old English poetry such as *Beowulf*. For much of his time in Leeds he worked on an alliterative poem on the *Children of Húrin*; late in 1924, or early in 1925, he put it aside and began two other alliterative poems, *The Flight of the Noldoli* and a *Lay of Éarendel*. Both were soon abandoned.

Return to Oxford

Early in 1925, after the retirement of Sir William Craigie, Rawlinson and Bosworth Professor of Anglo-Saxon, the chair was advertised for election. Tolkien applied.

It soon became clear to the electors that the choice was between Tolkien and his former tutor, Kenneth Sisam.

Sisam was a man of formidable industry and hard-nosed scholarship, who was moreover only four years Tolkien's senior; like Tolkien, he had once been on the staff of the *Dictionary*. Professional relations between them had not always been easy; Sisam's job at the University Press had involved nagging authors, amongst them Tolkien, for overdue texts and the abridgement of overlong ones. Sisam's work was close-hauled, bone-dry, and fiercely restricted to the text; Tolkien, although he was in his own way quite as rigorous, was always open to the larger imaginative and conjectural picture the details of the text suggested. If Sisam was in approach the classic, Tolkien was the romantic.

There were six electors for the Chair; three voted for Tolkien, and three for Sisam: the Vice-Chancellor gave his casting vote for Tolkien. On 21st July 1925, then, Tolkien was elected to the Rawlinson and Bosworth Chair of Anglo-Saxon at Oxford.

This was a remarkable achievement for a man of his years; to gain an Oxford chair, even so comparatively junior and recent a creation as that of Anglo-Saxon, aged only thirty-three argues a very unusual quality in him. He was unusual also in his religion: he joined the very few Catholic dons then at Oxford.

The prestige of his new job was high; its pay was not (the

stipend was £1,000 a year). To meet the growing expenses of school fees (the Tolkiens now had three children, aged eight, five, and one; their fourth and last, Priscilla, was born in 1929) and doctors' bills (Edith was often unwell), not to mention normal household expenses, Tolkien took on work as an external examiner for other universities, setting and marking papers. This was drudge's work, but remained a financial necessity for many years; Tolkien devoted large parts of the University vacations to it.

Oxford and Storytelling

Tolkien's day job was teaching English language by lectures, one-to-one tutorials, and tireless campaigning to preserve and, if possible, advance philological studies. He was constantly reading and re-reading the great monuments of the English tradition, both pre-Conquest and medieval, and their analogues amongst the literature of the North, notably Norse and Icelandic texts. From this rich mental soil, alongside his purely academic work, grew two sorts of creative writing: improvised stories for his children, and the high legendary matter of his 'elvish' tales. It took a decade or more, but eventually these two genera cross-fertilised, and produced a third thing both like and unlike themselves.

Meanwhile, Tolkien now held a senior post in country's oldest University; he was kept, and kept himself, very busy. For his first term, indeed, he was also teaching at Leeds. Tolkien was notable for his extensive preparation for his lectures; frequently, before lecturing on a particular text, he would prepare a new edition of it reflecting his own views of its nature and the problems it exhibited. This was both time-consuming and unusually diligent.

Tolkien had put aside the alliterative *Children of Húrin* before leaving Leeds; he began, now, *The Lay of Leithian*, a retelling of the Beren and Lúthien story in octosyllabic couplets. He worked on this, on and off, for the next six years.

Early in 1926, Tolkien wrote a short prose text, 'A Sketch of the Mythology', to give background to *The Lay of Leithian* and *The Children of Húrin* when they were sent to one of his old schoolmasters for comment. Originally meant purely as a synopsis, the 'Sketch' now became the primary prose vehicle for the development of Tolkien's legendarium; the original *Lost Tales* were put side, and never revised further. This synopsis, many years and layers of development later, became the book we know as *The Silmarillion*.

Unlike the *Lost Tales*, the 'Sketch' has no narrative framework explaining how these stories came to be told; it was to be some time before Tolkien was to find the necessary middle term between the high matter of his mythology and the grounded experience of the English reader. It was not made easier by the fact that Tolkien showed his writing to very few. Tolkien needed a properly appreciative audience.

Heavy Lewis

On 11th May 1926, at an English faculty meeting, Tolkien met Magdalen's recently elected Tutorial Fellow in English, a Belfast atheist, frustrated philosopher and aspirant poet named CS Lewis - 'Jack' to his intimates; to his undergraduate contemporaries, on account of his earnest intensity, 'Heavy Lewis'. Lewis noted in his diary that evening that Tolkien was "a smooth, pale, fluent little chap…No harm in him: only needs a smack or two."[10]

The previous term, in an effort to win allies for his proposal to admit more Old and Middle English literature into the syllabus at the expense of nineteenth century texts, Tolkien had organised a reading club for dons, to work through the major Icelandic sagas. It was called the Coalbiters (from the Norse *kolbítar*, those who sit so close to the fire that they 'bite the coal'). At some stage, someone invited Lewis to come along; he soon became a regular attendee, but his acquaintance with Tolkien only ripened into friendship late in 1929, when, at last, Lewis realised that Tolkien shared the same visceral enthusiasm for Norse mythology and William Morris as he did. They were also both fond of beer and tobacco, and of country walks.

Soon Tolkien lent Lewis the manuscript of *The Lay of Leithian*; Lewis was enthusiastic, with some quibbling over detail. Tolkien read him some of his prose narratives; he was more enthusiastic still. Tolkien wrote, many years later, that Lewis "was for long my only audience. Only from him did I ever get the idea that my 'stuff' could be more than a private hobby"; this encouragement, Tolkien said, was "the unpayable debt that I owe to him."[11]

The debt was not wholly one-sided; on 19th September 1931, Lewis had a long night talk with Tolkien and their friend Hugo Dyson which was instrumental in Lewis beginning to accept the 'myth of Christ' as true.

Stories told to my children

Tolkien's children were another and different spur to his imagination. He made up stories for them, often incorporating their favourite toys, or unusual places or things they saw whilst on holiday. Most of these were ephemeral, and have not survived; others were written down, and eventually published. Here, the key to the eventual emergence of his mythological writing was found.

The earliest stories to survive are a series of letters written to the Tolkien children from, it was feigned, Father Christmas. These began in 1920, when John Tolkien was three, and continued each year until 1943, when Priscilla, the youngest child, was fourteen. They were increasingly elaborate, and copiously illustrated: Tolkien was a very competent amateur artist in pencil, ink, chalk and watercolour. Another story began as an effort to console his son Michael after he lost a toy dog on holiday at Filey on the Yorkshire coast, in September 1925. It was written down by 1927, but not published, as *Roverandom*, until 1998. 1928 brought *Mr Bliss*, an illustrated story giving the adventures of some of his children's favourite toys (bears and a clockwork car). It was published only in 1982.

Around this time Tolkien wrote, also, an early version of *Farmer Giles of Ham*; this began as a story explaining Oxfordshire place-names. It was expanded and rewritten several times over the next decade.

In about 1930, sitting at his desk marking exam papers, Tolkien had the happy experience of finding the last page of a script left blank. On that blank page, he wrote "In a hole in the ground lived a hobbit."

Much ink has been spilt debating the origins of this sentence. Tolkien said it came to him from nowhere, and it is simplest to believe him. Soon, a story grew around that sentence, and parts of it were told to the Tolkien children during the early 1930s.

Work and the Legendarium

Tolkien was undoubtedly prodigal with help and advice to other scholars, as a glance at the prefaces to most works of scholarship in his field published during this time shows. Throughout his academic career, his influence was much wider than the list of his own scholarly publications would suggest. He was also busy trying to expand the philological element in the Oxford English course; with the help of Lewis and other allies, he had, for a time at least, some success in this.

At roughly this time, he wrote two longish poems, the *New Lay of the Völsungs* and the *New Lay of Gudrún* (which he usually called by the Old Norse names *Völsungakviða en nýja* and *Guðrúnakviða en nýja*) to fill up long-debated lacunae in the extant legends; this was a fine intersection between professional philology and his private endeavours. It was utterly characteristic of Tolkien's unconventional approach that he thought the best way to resolve textual cruces was to write another poetic treatment of the subject; it was also, unfortunately, one that was unlikely to gain wide acceptance amongst his scholarly peers. Work on these poems probably replaced that on the *Lay of Leithian*, which he laid aside in September 1931.

Tolkien also revised and expanded the 1926 sketch of the mythology; finished in 1930, with the title *Quenta Noldorinwa* ('the history of the Noldor'), it was the only version of the 'Silmarillion' narrative tradition ever fully completed. It was deliberately conceived as a compendium or summary of stories that, at least notionally, were told in a fuller form elsewhere.

Domestic troubles

Tolkien's professional life, then, was busy, and his imaginative writing varied and prolific; his personal life, though, was not easy. There were difficulties in his marriage; Edith had never settled into the social life of Oxford dons' wives, and was not part of Tolkien's circle of (male) friends. Tolkien was usually out for much of the day, and often in the evenings also. She was lonely, and felt neglected by her husband. She had had no particular preparation for running the large household she now had (four children, plus domestic help) and tended to cloak uncertainty with authoritarianism. Money was tight, even with Tolkien's constant work as an examiner; Edith's health was often precarious (she suffered from debilitating headaches, and chronic back pain) and doctors' bills were another worry. Also there was religion: Edith came to feel that Tolkien had unfairly pressured her into becoming a Catholic, and she resented this, particularly as her experience of Anglicanism in the years they were apart had been a happy and sociable one. She stopped practising as a Catholic, and was unhappy that Tolkien took the children to church; occasionally, she let her resentment spill over into anger. Tolkien himself kept an emotional loyalty to the faith of his childhood, and was grieved by what he saw as Edith's desertion of it. Nevertheless, amidst the quarrels, there was both forgiveness and enduring affection; although their domestic life was not always exactly happy. Tolkien wrote in his diary, on 1st October 1933, "Friendship with Lewis compensates for much."[12] In 1934, Fr Francis Morgan died aged seventy-seven. Hearing this news, Tolkien said to Lewis, "I feel like a lost survivor into a new alien world after the real world has passed away."[13]

The Inklings

Some time in the mid-1930s, an informal literary and discussion club was started by Lewis, centred around him and his friends. They borrowed the name of a defunct undergraduate literary society, 'The Inklings'. Tolkien was one of the original circle. They met every week or two during term time, and listened to one or more of their number read from a work-in-progress. This was followed by general talk, often until the small hours. Later, they also met one morning a week to drink beer in, usually, The Eagle and Child pub on St Giles; in fact, Tolkien and Lewis had since the late 1920s met regularly for talk over beer; this opened their meetings to a wider circle.

A deal of over-solemn analysis of this group has been written. The Inklings was, above all else, a collection of Lewis's friends; his friends, by and large, were interesting men, educated, curious, with (in some cases great) literary talent, and overwhelmingly Christian. Like most 'writers' groups', their main function was as an audience, to listen and criticise and encourage. For a writer to have a regular and sympathetic but not uncritical audience is an unmeasurable boon. It was part of Lewis's gift for friendship that he could coax quite disparate people, and some like Tolkien who were shy of making their work public, to engage in such an enterprise. If the Inklings did nothing else, its function as partial midwife for *The Lord of the Rings* would mark it as a significant literary phenomenon.

A Wilderness of Dragons
- *Beowulf* and *The Hobbit*

Reclaiming *Beowulf*

In 1936, Tolkien gave a lecture which revolutionised the study of the Old English poem *Beowulf*. He had been lecturing on *Beowulf* every year since he was appointed to his Oxford chair, and had taught countless classes and individual students. His sense of what *Beowulf* was, and his sympathy for the temper and manner of its author, had grown and developed enormously. He was given the chance to summarise this for a broader audience when he was invited to give a prestigious British Academy lecture. His paper was called 'Beowulf: the Monsters and the Critics'; and no one afterwards has been able to read the poem in the same way.

Beowulf, he argued, must be read not as a quarry for other things, but as a poem by a Christian: one who lived in the shadow of the old paganism, and who felt nostalgia for and a sympathy with those who had died according to its bleak, defiant code. This code, which Tolkien called "the Northern theory of courage", may be crisply summarised as the claim that (in Tom Shippey's words) "defeat is no refutation"; even if all human endeavour is finally doomed to end in decay and failure, if (as Norse legend said) at the end even the gods will be defeated by the powers of evil, nevertheless it was still right to fight for truth, and loyalty, and honour, even (perhaps especially) without hope of victory or reward. The 'monsters' - the ogres Grendel and his mother, and the dragon that is Beowulf's bane - are proper opponents for a man in this setting.

The Hobbit - style and sources

Tolkien lent the unfinished manuscript of *The Hobbit* to a former student; she passed it to a friend, who worked for the publisher George Allen & Unwin. She in turn strongly suggested the story be finished and submitted for publication; and this Tolkien did in late 1936. The firm's chairman, Stanley Unwin, paid his ten-year-old son Rayner a shilling to report on the book; Rayner liked it, and Unwin agreed to publish. Unwin was an unlikely partner for Tolkien; he was a non-smoking, teetotal pacifist and Nonconformist of distinctly left-wing views: he and Tolkien would have disagreed on pretty much everything. Nevertheless, Unwin was a canny businessman, and recognised a classic when he saw one. In September 1937, *The Hobbit* was published; Tolkien was forty-five.

The story had started, as we saw, at Tolkien's desk some years earlier during his annual chore of exam marking. As usual with him, a name gave rise to a story; it soon attracted to itself further names from Tolkien's professional life.

The dwarves, and the wizard Gandalf, come from the *Elder Edda*, in a list (the *Dvergatal*) usually dismissed as a meaningless rigmarole; Tolkien decided it in fact preserved the roster of a famous quest for lost treasure. Mirkwood came straight from primitive Gothia; the dragon, Smaug, is of the lineage of the drakes of Beowulf and Sigurðr. This cross-fertilisation of names brought with it, perhaps inevitably, a similar cross-fertilisation of theme: most readers of *The Hobbit* notice how, as the story progresses, it becomes by degrees more serious until, at its end, with the debates before the Lonely Mountain and the Battle of the Five Armies, it approaches the high seriousness and brusque moral complexity of Icelandic saga.

There was another source, too, besides Tolkien's philological day job; names and characters and settings from Tolkien's legendarium (Gondolin, Elrond, the Elvenking in his halls) found their way into the story, and gave it another layer of resonance and what Tolkien called 'depth': the sense of untold stories and half-seen vistas at the edge of the tale. This not only had implications for Tolkien's literary technique; it also meant that hobbits were now a tangential part of his legendarium. This was to have tremendous consequences for his writing.

Meanwhile, Tolkien began writing a fine manuscript copy of the *Quenta Silmarillion*, incorporating all the numerous revisions he had made to the tales since the *Quenta Noldorinwa* of 1930.

Tolkien recalled years later a conversation with Lewis about speculative fiction in which both lamented the lack of the sort of books they liked to read; Lewis proposed they make good this lack themselves. Lewis took space travel as his theme, Tolkien time-travel. In Lewis's case, this led directly to the first of his science fiction novels, *Out of the Silent Planet* (in which Tolkien appears, thinly disguised, as the philologist Elwin Ransom). Tolkien, characteristically, was more elaborate and piecemeal in his efforts. In the years 1936-1937 he drafted parts of a story called *The Lost Road*, in which a father and son pair are traced backwards through successive ages from the present to a time of myth, where the recurring theme of a 'lost road' to the uttermost west finds its proper exemplar in the downfall of Númenor, Tolkien's Atlantis. This was done, in part, to exorcise a recurrent dream of a great wave drowning a sunlit land that Tolkien had experienced since childhood. *The Lost Road* was never completed; Tolkien returned to the theme a decade later.

They asked for a sequel

The Hobbit was an immediate success, and Tolkien's publisher was eager for more. He asked Tolkien to write a sequel. Tolkien was not unwilling, but asked Unwin if he would like to consider any of the stories he had already written. Unwin was happy to do so; so, in mid-November 1937, Tolkien met him in London and gave him a large bundle of manuscripts. These included versions of *Farmer Giles of Ham* and *Mr Bliss*, and the unfinished *Lost Road*; most importantly for Tolkien, however, he also included the unfinished long poem, *The Lay of Leithian*, and the fine manuscript of the *Quenta Silmarillion*, comprising the first two-thirds of the text (the remaining third, as yet unrevised, was not included). All of this was given to a publisher's reader named Edward Crankshaw to be assessed: apart from, it seems, the *Silmarillion* itself.

Crankshaw confessed himself puzzled by the poem, but very impressed by the few pages of the prose *Silmarillion* he had been given to read as background. These few pages were all he saw, however; for some reason, the full text as it had been given to Unwin was withheld. Crankshaw did not feel able to recommend any of the texts he had seen should be published; Unwin conveyed this to Tolkien on 16th December, with the hope that *The Silmarillion* might be the source for further stories like *The Hobbit*. Understandably, Tolkien was under the misapprehension that *The Silmarillion* had been read in full before being rejected, but took comfort from what he mistakenly interpreted as the general approval of it. The result was unexpected to both sides:

"They wanted a sequel. But I wanted heroic legends and high romance. The result was *The Lord of the Rings*."[14]

There is, of course, no knowing what might have happened if Crankshaw had been given the whole

Silmarillion to read, or if it had been published; but it is utterly certain that, if it had been accepted in 1937, the sequel to *The Hobbit* would have been very different. The rejection of the 1937 *Silmarillion* was the direct cause of *The Lord of the Rings* in its eventual form; it was also the main reason *The Silmarillion* was never completed.

The Lord of the Rings

Tolkien began the 'new Hobbit' the same year the original was published, in fact by 19th December 1937. It was not finished until twelve years later, and not published for another six after that.

The tale grew in the telling

Tolkien made several unsatisfactory drafts of the first chapters between December 1937 and March 1938; then he laid the book aside until August 1938, and worked solidly between then and February 1939; for the rest of 1939, although he told his publisher he hoped to finish the story by mid-June, he worked on it only in desultory fashion, not helped by the uncertainties of wartime, and by a head injury that left him concussed and unwell for some months.

In this fallow interval, he gave a lecture 'On Fairy Stories' we will discuss later; and also wrote *Leaf by Niggle*, an allegory of the creative life and its frustrations and hopes.

In September 1939 the staff of the University Press's London office moved to Oxford; amongst them was an editor called Charles Williams. Williams was a prolific writer of 'spiritual thrillers' and an exponent of romantic theology (that is, human love as an authentic route to knowing God) in what he reckoned was the style of Dante. He was also a confirmed dabbler in the occult. Lewis had read some of his work, Williams had read Lewis's *Allegory of Love* in proof, and they had exchanged admiring letters. Now that Williams was living in Oxford, Lewis quickly incorporated him in his circle of friends, and this included meetings of the Inklings. He also got Williams permission to give lectures at the university. Very obviously Williams, rather than Tolkien, was now the primary object of Lewis's enthusiasm. Tolkien was a sensitive man, and quickly noticed. Lewis professed to believe that closeness to one friend does not diminish with the arrival of another; but Tolkien, and I suspect most of us, would disagree. It is difficult to have two best friends simultaneously. Lewis's friends were now expected to join in Lewis's admiration for Williams's writing. This Tolkien was temperamentally unable to do; he liked Williams, but found his books baffling and distasteful by turns. This marks the first stage in the decline of Tolkien's relations with Lewis. Williams died suddenly in May 1945, after a supposedly routine operation; but the damage was done.

Tolkien took up *The Lord of Rings* again in August 1940, and wrote steadily until term started in October. Then he put it aside until the Christmas vacation; throughout 1941, he worked intermittently until, by the end of the year, the story had reached Lothlórien. By the end of January 1942, he had drafted the first four chapters of Book III. He then laid the work aside for the rest of the academic year. The Long (summer) Vacation of 1942 gave him time to write the remaining chapters of Book III. Then he stopped, and wrote nothing more for almost eighteen months. He did not tackle Book IV (Frodo and Sam's journey to Mordor) until April 1944; by the end of May, it was done. He began Book V that October; during the next two university terms and vacation, he managed some sporadic work. After March 1945, however, he did nothing more to the book until September of the following year: 'real life' made a violent intervention.

Distractions

On 26th January 1945, the Merton Professor of English Language, HC Wyld, died. The Merton chairs were older, more prestigious, and better paid than Tolkien's position. They also came with a Fellowship at Merton, one of the richer and physically more agreeable colleges, certainly compared to Tolkien's then college, Pembroke. He was unofficially sounded out whether he wished to be considered for the job. He decided he did. In the meantime, as one of the two surviving professors in the English School, proportionately more administrative work devolved on Tolkien. This, and the normal business of term-time (lectures, tutorials, supervision of graduate students, interminable meetings of college and faculty), meant no leisure for writing.

At the end of May, the electors to the Merton chair agreed to offer it to Tolkien. A month later, on 23rd June, he was formally elected; his new job began with the academic year, that October. He had now, at the age of fifty-three, reached the highest position open to an English scholar of philology: he was the undisputed head of his profession. In the short term, however, this was more a burden than anything else, as he had to cover, in addition to his new responsibilities, those of his former chair as well. Procedural delays meant that a new professor of Anglo-Saxon was not appointed until April 1946, to begin work that October. Tolkien in effect did two jobs for a whole year.

At the end of 1945 and the start of 1946, during this hiatus in the writing of *The Lord of the Rings*, he began *The Notion Club Papers*. This recasts *The Lost Road* of the previous decade, and rather improves on it; but, as so often, it was unfinished. Tolkien wrote it at a furious pace over Christmas 1945, presumably meaning to finish before the academic term started, and also (perhaps) to reassure himself that his creative powers had not been permanently affected by his failure (as it seemed) to complete *The Lord of the Rings*. The strain of this, after a term of double workload, was simply too much, and his health gave way.

That February, Tolkien's eldest son, John, was ordained priest. Tolkien served his first Mass, in the church of St Aloysius, Oxford.

In the middle of March 1946, Tolkien's doctor ordered him to rest for six months to avoid a complete physical collapse; in the event, he spent three weeks at Stonyhurst, where the English College students (John Tolkien amongst them) had been quartered during the war. This was hardly the six months off he had been prescribed; the rest did him some good, though, enough to carry him through the remainder of the academic year.

At the end of June 1946, the other Merton chair, in English Literature, also fell vacant; its occupant had reached retirement age. This meant, for the time being, yet more administrative work for Tolkien; it also involved him in selecting a successor. Tolkien's preferred candidate was CS Lewis, a natural choice for the vacancy; but he was passed over, in large part (it seems) because some of the electors were suspicious of Lewis's activities as a Christian apologist.

It was not until September 1946 that Tolkien again took up the manuscript of *The Lord of the Rings*. He returned to Book V, which was finished by the end of October 1947, and also revised Books I and II.[15] There was another interruption early in 1947. On 14th March, Tolkien, Edith and Priscilla left their house in Northmoor Road, where the children had grown up but which was now too large and too expensive for only three people, and moved to a small Merton College house in Manor Road. Uprooting from a house they had occupied for twenty years was physically disruptive, leaving aside the sentimental wrench of leaving a much-loved family home. Inevitably, some of Tolkien's papers were lost during the move.

At the end of the 1948 summer vacation, Tolkien went to his son Michael's house in Woodcote (Michael was away on holiday) to try to finish *The Lord of the Rings*. There, between 14th August and 14th September, he completed a draft of Book VI. Soon afterwards, the academic year began again. The complete work was revised, and typed up, by October 1949.

Finished, at last

In some ways, *The Lord of the Rings* underwent something of the same transformation as *The Hobbit*; as Tolkien wrote, the story became increasingly drawn into the web of stories that was the *Silmarillion* material, which became, in fact, the ancient history of Middle Earth. *The Lord of the Rings* became the elegiac conclusion to a long history, the final episode in the gradual fading of elvish things from the world. Here, as in *The Hobbit*, allusions throughout the text and appendices give an impression of 'depth', only to a far greater extent.

One critical difference between *The Lord of the Rings* and the earlier *Silmarillion* stories is the presence of hobbits. They function not only as a vehicle for Tolkien to express his love for a vanished (and idealised) rural England, but also as a 'way in' for the reader unfamiliar with the high literary modes of romance, myth and epic. Tolkien's story values deeply unfashionable qualities (nobility, loyalty, self-sacrifice, ceremoniousness); but we see these qualities, mostly, through the eyes of the hobbits, whose initial reactions may mirror our own, but who allow us to enter into these themes, as they do, without cynicism or irony.

As in *The Hobbit*, but on a greater scale, Tolkien drew on his professional interests for *The Lord of the Rings*. Most obviously, the Rohirrim are an idealised portrait of early Anglo-Saxons (specifically, early Mercians), who speak West Midland-accented Old English, and exemplify Old English customs and habits, including the 'Northern theory of courage' described in Tolkien's *Beowulf* lecture.

However, although it is possible to discern sources for elements in *The Lord of the Rings*, it is not necessarily helpful to itemise them, as if that explained how they work in the finished book; Tolkien integrated elements from a wide variety of sources both literary and personal into a story that functions on its own terms. Thinking that by identifying the source of a particular theme or passage or event we have thus understood or explained it, is to fall into exactly the same mistake Tolkien complained of in the critics of *Beowulf*.

CS Lewis had been unstinting in his encouragement and praise of *The Lord of the Rings* as it was read to the Inklings, or passed to him privately; Tolkien however was less enthusiastic about Lewis's own 'big book', the sixteenth-century volume of the *Oxford History of English Literature*, which was also slowly gestating during these years.[16] Tolkien took strong objection to Lewis's estimation of St Thomas More, and to other aspects of the book which he felt illustrated Lewis's visceral anti-Catholicism. Lewis had also begun his Narnia stories for children, and read parts to Tolkien; Tolkien detested them. Nevertheless, Lewis published them, with great success.

But who would publish?

The Lord of the Rings had been written in response to Stanley Unwin's request for a sequel, which Unwin had hoped might appear within a year or two. Now, twelve years later, it was actually finished, Tolkien needed to get it published. It took five years for this to happen.

Late in 1949, Unwin finally published *Farmer Giles of Ham*. It sold only slowly, and Tolkien was not convinced of their enthusiasm for his work, still less for the now finished *Lord of the Rings*. Increasingly, Tolkien wanted *The Silmarillion* published at the same time; only thus, he reckoned, could the mass of allusions within the text to his legendarium be made sense of.

One of the Inklings, the Dominican Fr Gervase Mathew, introduced Tolkien to Milton Waldman, a Catholic who worked as an adviser to the publisher Collins. Late in 1949, Waldman was given the completed *Lord of the Rings* to read. In the new year, he told Tolkien he wanted to publish both *The Lord of the Rings* and *The Silmarillion* if Tolkien had no 'moral or legal' commitment to Unwin. Tolkien asked Stanley Unwin to publish both books; Unwin told him it would be difficult and expensive, but not impossible. At the start of April, he sent Tolkien a copy of a report written by his son, Rayner, who had seen *The Lord of the Rings* but not *The Silmarillion*. Rayner recommended incorporating anything essential from *The Silmarillion* into *The Lord of the Rings*, if necessary by cutting material from the latter; or, if Tolkien would not entertain this, publishing *The Lord of the Rings* and, "after having a second look at it", "dropping" *The Silmarillion*. Tolkien was furious, and was baffled why Unwin had thought showing him Rayner's letter might be helpful. He insisted Unwin answer his flat question: would he publish *The Lord of the Rings* and *The Silmarillion* together, both uncut? Not unnaturally (since he had never seen a completed typescript of the latter - in fact, one did not then exist) Unwin refused, as Tolkien must have known he would, in a letter dated 17th April 1950. Tolkien then approached Milton Waldman, who invited him to London to discuss publication. Waldman bluntly told him *The*

Lord of the Rings was too long. Nevertheless, Tolkien still meant to publish both works together.

The Silmarillion Renewed

If Tolkien was to hope to publish *The Silmarillion*, it needed to be set in order and, for the most part, largely revised, both in light of how his mythology had developed since the previous draft, and also to make sure it was congruent with *The Lord of the Rings*. His earlier revisions in 1937 had not covered the whole text, and had been abandoned when, as Tolkien understood it, the book had been rejected. Typically, Tolkien did not complete the earlier revision, but started again at the beginning of the work, and reached roughly the same point as he had in 1937 before, some time in 1951, again laying the work aside. At the same time, he began to rewrite the three 'Great Tales' of the legendarium on ampler scale, from which, he planned, the latter parts of the eventual *Silmarillion* would derive.

For the story of Beren and Lúthien, he had already started to rewrite the old *Lay of Leithian*; the rewritten text forms no more than one sixth of the original four thousand lines of rhyming couplets; and even that, we should remember, did not complete the story. At the same time, he began a prose version of the same tale; it did not proceed very far. In 1951, he began an extended prose saga of *The Fall of Gondolin*; sadly, he never finished it. He also began a long and ambitious prose version of the Túrin story, the *Narn i*

Chîn Húrin (*Tale of the Children of Húrin*). This, too, was set aside incomplete. All three of the long versions of the Great Tales, then, were stalled in their revision; this meant that, in effect, the last third or so of the *Silmarillion* text was also stalled, since Tolkien intended to derive it from the longer Tales.

Lit and Lang, again

In 1951, the perennial dispute over the Oxford English syllabus came to one of its periodic crises. The new holders of the professorial chairs were, unlike Tolkien and Lewis, keen for the academic study of Victorian literature to be restored to the syllabus, inevitably at the expense of philological concerns. Tolkien was appointed to the committee to consider this; he was persuaded to support the majority view, and recommend the syllabus he and Lewis had fought hard for should be replaced. Lewis was appalled, and at once badgered Tolkien to change his mind; when the new syllabus came to a general vote, Tolkien sided with Lewis in opposing it. It passed, despite their opposition.[17]

This, in some ways, marks the start of what Tom Shippey has called 'the long defeat' of academic philology. Professional matters were not going wholly Tolkien's way; nor, it seemed, were his literary efforts. Negotiations with Collins over *The Lord of the Rings* first stalled, then petered out entirely; Waldman was often away, and his colleagues were not sympathetic to Tolkien's work. Tolkien would not settle for an abridgement; which looked like meaning no book at all.

Return to Unwin

In November 1951, and again in June 1952, Rayner Unwin wrote to Tolkien, enquiring about *The Lord of the Rings* and *The Silmarillion*; Tolkien asked if Unwin were still interested in the book: "Can anything be done… to unlock gates I slammed myself?" Rayner Unwin was given the book to read, and advised his father it should be published, even at a loss. In November 1952, Stanley Unwin offered to publish the book, on a profit-sharing basis (which meant that Tolkien received no royalties until the publishers' costs were covered, but thereafter a half-share of the profits: if the book sold well, he would benefit much more than under a normal royalty agreement). Tolkien accepted.

In 1954, CS Lewis was elected to a new professorial chair in Cambridge; he left Oxford after almost thirty years, and a series of disappointment over jobs - he had been passed over for three separate Oxford professorships in quick succession. Although he still lived in Oxford at the weekends, this meant that he saw less of Tolkien, although their days of close friendship had been over for a decade. There was also, as we shall see, a woman.

Between July 1953 and mid-1955, Tolkien was busy with proofs of *The Lord of the Rings*, which (he had conceded, reluctantly) was to be published serially, in three volumes. The first volume, *The Fellowship of the Ring*, was published on 29th July 1954, and the second, *The Two Towers*, on 11th November that same year. There was then a delay of almost a year before the final volume was published, as Tolkien scrambled to complete the Appendices which, in the absence of the full *Silmarillion*, he saw as the irreducible minimum of additional information needed to make the book comprehensible. Inevitably, he produced more material than there was space for, and a good deal had to be dropped; he also abandoned a promised index. Finally, on 20th October 1955, the last volume, *The Return of the King*, was published.

Tolkien was apprehensive: "I have exposed my heart to be shot at."[18] Some of Tolkien's colleagues at Oxford were privately, or not so privately, suspicious that he had written *The Lord of the Rings* in time that would have been better spent on proper scholarship. It is indisputably true that Tolkien was capable of writing a big and important book on English philology, and never did so; and that the vast intellectual efforts and energies expended on his legendarium must in part be to blame.

Despite Tolkien's apprehension, and his publisher's caution, *The Lord of the Rings* was a success from the start; when American editions of it appeared in the mid-

1960s, his fame became global, and seems likely to be enduring (he is repeatedly, and by a long chalk, voted the 'best author' in polls). What marks him off from his hordes of imitators is, precisely, philology: the fact that his imaginary world is deeply rooted in language, in names and words with their own inner consistency, meaning and resonance, which have in fact given rise to that world, is in the best and broadest sense a philological one, and is (I would suggest) the key to his success. Whilst philology was defeated in the academy, outside, amongst people who read books for enjoyment, it has won a stupendous victory, although probably most of Tolkien's readers are unaware of it.

In 1956, preparation began of the *Jerusalem Bible*, an English version of the great monument of French Biblical scholarship, the *Bible de Jérusalem*. Its general editor, Fr Alexander Jones, assembled a mixed bag of writers to produce the text. He approached Tolkien, who agreed to help. Tolkien produced a complete draft of the Book of Jonah, although it is unclear how closely the published text reflects his work; he may also have drafted some other texts, but in a more fragmentary form. In the event, pressure of work meant he was unable to do as much as he, or Jones, had supposed; at one stage Jones seems to have hoped Tolkien would agree, after his retirement in 1959, to act as literary editor for the whole project, but that scheme came to nothing.

Breach with Lewis

There had been growing distance between Tolkien and Lewis since, at least, 1940, when Charles Williams had arrived in Oxford. As we have seen, professional matters, not uninfluenced by religious difference, introduced further tension between them, and in 1954 Lewis left Oxford altogether. The gradual decay of friendship is one thing; a positive breach is another, and that came with Lewis's unexpected marriage.

The sentimentalised version of the story told by the 1993 film *Shadowlands* is not wholly accurate. Joy Gresham (née Davidman) was an American divorcée who had corresponded with Lewis for some years, and who had moved to England with her sons. Lewis's brother, together with other observers, was convinced she had set her cap at Lewis: "It was obvious what was going to happen." Early in 1956, the Home Office declined to renew her visa; by now, her sons were at school (the fees paid by Lewis) and she was living within walking distance of Lewis's house. Lewis agreed to a civil marriage to allow her to stay in the country; it took place on 23rd April 1956. They continued to live apart; in October, she was diagnosed with incurable cancer, and Lewis discovered he was in love with her. They were married on 21st March 1957. Soon afterwards, her cancer went into remission.[19]

Tolkien did not find out about Lewis's marriage until eight months after the event, when he read a notice of it in

The Times; he could not approve of marriage to a divorced woman, but was mostly hurt to have been kept wholly in the dark. Their intimacy was now decidedly past; apart from anything else, Lewis was in Cambridge four nights each week. But the other breaches between them were deeper than physical distance, and less easily remedied.

Last Years

In 1959, Tolkien retired, aged sixty-seven. *The Lord of the Rings* was an established success; his public was eager for more; he now had, presumably, leisure. What, now, was to prevent him from finishing *The Silmarillion*, his long-prepared legendarium?

In the event, he published nothing else on the matter of Middle Earth during his lifetime.

Delays and frustrations

To understand why, we need to look at the state of the work by the late 1950s. Little had been done to most of the material since the 1937 *Quenta Silmarillion* had been put aside when Tolkien began work on the 'Hobbit sequel'. He had revised some parts of it in the early 1950s, when he had hoped Collins would publish it alongside *The Lord of the Rings*, but much of his effort went into writing extended versions of the three 'Great Tales', all abandoned unfinished, rather than the *Silmarillion* proper (which, he had decided, could be done only after the Great Tales were fixed). Most of the stories were in a state of confusion, with in some cases multiple partly-revised versions in existence, and in others (such as the famous, and central, *Fall of Gondolin*) nothing later the original 1917 *Book of Lost Tales*. At every turn, his efforts at reducing this mass of text to order met with knotty problems of consistency, of nomenclature, of (in some cases) philosophical and theological uncertainty. Resolving these questions was at least as likely to lead to his beginning a wholly new text, whether story or discursive essay, as to connected revision of the existing material. Even had his time been otherwise uninterrupted and tranquil, untangling all this would have been a stiff task for a man approaching his eighth decade. And of course, Tolkien's life, like anyone else's, never contained only the problems and tasks of his choosing. Interruptions came thick and fast.

One problem was a series of physical dislocations. When Tolkien retired as Professor of English Language, he also had to give up his rooms as Fellow of Merton. This meant finding room to house the thousands of books and other material he had kept there. Some of his library was dispersed; the remainder ended up in the garage attached to his house in Headington. Then there was the unavoidable human condition. Edith had been in poor health for years; Tolkien, too, was often ill, and both were now old. There were other books, long-promised and long overdue, to be finished: an edition of a medieval text, *Ancrene Wisse*, begun in 1935, was finally and after much labour and frustration published in 1962, in time for Tolkien's seventieth birthday. For two terms in 1962-63, Tolkien came out of retirement to cover for his successor in the chair of Anglo-Saxon, who was in America on leave.

The effects of all this on *The Silmarillion* cannot be measured simply in terms of time expended; anyone who has ever worked on a complex intellectual project knows that, if it is put aside for some time, it cannot be resumed without considerable mental effort re-familiarising oneself with the problems involved. These are the customary perils of the scholarly life, of course; but this does not make them any less real in any given case.

Another problem was the lack of an audience. The role CS Lewis played in encouraging and accompanying the gestation of *The Lord of the Rings* can hardly be overstated; Tolkien, as we have seen, saw clearly that without him it would never have been finished. Now, however, Tolkien had been estranged from Lewis for some years, and had found no one able to take his place, as audience, sympathetic critic, general encourager.[20] Tolkien essayed various schemes to have one or another of his American fans help prepare *The Silmarillion*, but none worked out as he hoped.

Perhaps this does something to balance the impression that Tolkien spent the next fourteen years doing crossword puzzles and doodling elvishly on newspapers. Like any of us, of course, Tolkien sometimes wasted time, and newspapers and crosswords were one of his relaxations; but the main reasons for delay were interruptions, dislocations, ill-health, and old age.

Revisions and Late-written works

We saw that completing the three Great Tales, of Túrin, Tuor, and Beren and Lúthien to his satisfaction was the necessary precursor to producing a final text of *The Silmarillion*. In the years 1958-60, he turned again to the *Narn i Chîn Húrin*, which was within striking distance of being finished. It never reached a fully satisfactory form, however; he now began another subsidiary text, to take up the unresolved elements of the *Narn* and incorporate them into the *Silmarillion* proper. The resulting text, *The Wanderings of Húrin*, is the last true narrative addition Tolkien made to his account of the Elder Days. From this period date, also, various shorter ancillary works clarifying particular issues now problematic or inconsistent in the light of the material already published. The sheer multitudinousness of the questions to be addressed and problems to be resolved must have seemed, often, overwhelming.

Perhaps some of this was 'displacement activity', tasks Tolkien undertook to occupy himself because he was unable to engage properly with the main problem at hand: how to make *The Silmarillion* work. Its component tales were all written in a high style, without the mediation provided in his published works by hobbits; there was, for the contemporary reader, no obvious 'way in'. For many years, Tolkien had tried variations on the device of an Anglo-Saxon seafarer as a 'framing device' for the stories, and a means of accounting for their transmission; latterly, he considered presenting them as tales 'translated from the Elvish' by Bilbo Baggins. But these resolutions themselves raised further questions, and he could settle on no satisfying answer to this conundrum; this in itself tended to make work on the central texts slow and difficult.

In 1960, in another distraction, he started a wholesale rewriting of *The Hobbit*; he had grown to regret the tone of much of the book, particularly its intrusive narrator, and decided to recast the story to make it stylistically more like *The Lord of the Rings*. After a few chapters, however, he became tangled in an unavailing attempt to make sense of the phases of the moon in the book, and put it aside.

1961 saw the publication of *The Adventures of Tom Bombadil*, collecting mostly older verse. The broadly comic aim of most of the pieces has probably masked the serious intent of some of them, particularly the last two, *Sea-Bell* and *The Last Ship*; although not new, they were for this collection given a newly elegiac cast. Tolkien felt that at some level his contact with faërie, with the sources of his inspiration, was now fading or uncertain.

On 22nd November 1963, CS Lewis died. He was only sixty-five. He had been ill with kidney problems for some time, and that July had almost died of a heart attack. He had resigned his job; by mid-November, his kidneys were failing. Death came suddenly, but hardly unexpectedly. Tolkien wrote to his daughter, "this feels like an axe-blow near the roots."[21] The following year, Lewis's posthumous work *Letters to Malcolm: Mainly on Prayer* appeared. Tolkien was appalled by it ("a distressing and in parts horrifying work");[22] he began an essay discussing Lewis's religious views, which (Tolkien was increasingly convinced) had been dominated by the Protestantism, or better anti-Catholicism, of his Ulster childhood. The essay was called 'The Ulsterior Motive'. It has never been published.

In the summer of 1966, Clyde Kilby, an American fan who was curator of the Tolkien and Lewis manuscripts at Wheaton College, Illinois, spent three months in Oxford helping Tolkien sort through the *Silmarillion* manuscripts. Kilby was struck by the sheer quantity and variety of the unpublished material:

> One can imagine the perplexity of a writer with so many ideas and so many incomplete or unperfected writings on hand and with the realisation of so little time left. He was then seventy-four.
>
> Two things immediately impressed me. One was that *The Silmarillion* would never be completed. The other was the size of my own task.[23]

In the event, whilst the visit doubtless helped to introduce a little more order to Tolkien's papers, it was both only a small start on a large problem, and was soon overtaken by further sources of entropy.

The short tale *Smith of Wootton Major* appeared in 1967; it is another minor work (it in fact began as an introduction, never finished, to a volume of George MacDonald), but one which again expresses Tolkien's sadness at what he saw as his exile from faërie.

In September and October of 1967 Tolkien was ill; his eldest son, Fr John Tolkien, came to stay with his parents, as he had several times before, to recover from nervous exhaustion. The following January, Edith's health failed owing, in great part, to the strain of looking after them.

Bournemouth

For some years Tolkien and Edith had taken holidays in Bournemouth, usually staying at the Miramar Hotel on the sea-front. This provided the sort of agreeable, unstuffy (and unbookish) society in which Edith flourished. She became very attached to their visits; in 1968, Tolkien decided they should move there permanently, to make some belated recompense to her for her years of loneliness amongst his friends and occupations in Oxford. They rather impulsively bought a bungalow a short distance from the hotel, and began, once more, to pack up and move house.

In mid-June, before they had moved from their Oxford house, Tolkien fell downstairs and broke his leg badly; he spent the next month in hospital. The contents of his study were packed and moved in his absence. The disruption to his books and papers was considerable; although not as much was actually lost as Tolkien feared, nevertheless this chaos, added to the shock of the injury, interrupted him when, at last, he had begun to make some progress with his writing. His wife was too frail properly to supervise the movers, and Tolkien's boxed books and papers were piled indiscriminately in the garage. When he left hospital, he and Edith spent another month living in the Miramar whilst their house was made ready. His leg was another month in plaster, and he was unable to walk without crutches or a stick for the rest of the year. His library and papers remained in chaos for months.

Edith was happy to be in Bournemouth, and regained something of the vivacity she had possessed as a young woman; Tolkien, although he took pleasure in his wife's happiness, felt isolated, cut off from the society of his intellectual peers. Friends visited occasionally, but it was not like living in Oxford.

Slowly, after his papers had finally been set in order, he began to write. As in 1958-60, however, rather than further work on *The Silmarillion* proper, he wrote a number of speculative treatises addressing particular questions from the legendarium; usually these began as philological investigations (sometimes in answer to readers' letters), but soon developed in philosophical, theological or simple narrative directions. Many of these texts survive only in more or less illegible manuscripts. This burst of creativity (Tolkien, remember, was now seventy-seven) was interrupted by illness. He resumed work in October 1969, and wrote a short text *Of Dwarves and Men*.

At the start of 1970, he complained to his son Michael that progress on *The Silmarillion* was slow, mostly confined to co-ordinating details of nomenclature, and constantly interrupted: Edith's health was poor, he was feeling his own age, and there was a constant press of 'business' and chores. He had no permanent secretary or domestic help. At the start of 1971, he made some revision and expansions to the *Silmarillion* chapter 'On Maeglin'. He did little for the rest of the year, and in October was ill again.

Oxford at last

On 29th November 1971, after ten days' illness, Edith Tolkien died. Tolkien was bereft; "she was (and knew she was) my Lúthien. But the story has gone crooked, and I am left, and I cannot plead before the inexorable Mandos."[24] He was not sure he could write again. Certainly, he did not want to stay in Bournemouth. He began to cast about for a house in Oxford.

In the 1972 New Year's Honours, Tolkien was appointed CBE; later that month, his son Christopher wrote unprompted to the Warden of Merton asking about college rooms for his father: the governing body unanimously voted Tolkien should be made a residential fellow. In mid-March, he moved to a flat in Merton Street, with a college scout and his wife to look after him. At the end of March, he went to the Palace to receive his CBE. He planned to resume writing, and publish *The Silmarillion* in instalments. In June, his rooms were burgled and his CBE medal, together with some of Edith's jewellery, was stolen. His papers remained in storage for some time; he wrote nothing, it seems, until that November. Thereafter he produced some brief discussions of particular points, often (as before) provoked by questions in readers' letters: on elvish reincarnation, wizards, and minor characters from the legendarium.

He was ill again at the start of 1973, with persistent and severe indigestion; his doctor banned wine and rich food. He wrote little or nothing other than letters. That summer, he wrote to a friend, "over and above all the afflictions and obstacles I have endured since *The Lord of the Rings* came out, I have lost confidence."[25] That year, he made a few notes in August, nothing more.

On August 28th, he was driven to Bournemouth to stay with friends. During the night of August 30th, after attending a birthday party, he was taken ill; a hospital diagnosed a bleeding gastric ulcer. Two of his children were abroad, but John and Priscilla came to Bournemouth at once. He seemed to be getting better; but the next day, September 1st, he developed a chest infection.

In the early hours of the following morning, Sunday 2nd September 1973, John Ronald Reuel Tolkien died. He was eighty-one years old.

Posthumous Publications

Tolkien's will named his third son, Christopher, who like his father was an English don at Oxford, as his literary executor. His immediate task was to see what could be done with his father's papers. Could the long-promised *Silmarillion* ever be published?

The Silmarillion

Tolkien had perhaps hoped to finish *The Silmarillion* in time for the Queen's Silver Jubilee in 1977; he still thought of it as dedicated "to England, to my country." In 1975 Christopher Tolkien resigned his Fellowship at New College to devote himself full-time to his father's estate. With the help of Guy Gavriel Kay (a Canadian law student, later himself a noted writer of quasi-historical fantasy fiction) he compiled the published *Silmarillion*. He was under considerable pressure from readers, his publisher, and his own sense of duty to produce a readable text quickly; inevitably, he made some editorial decisions that, with hindsight and leisure, might have been made otherwise. But the nature of the component texts would hardly admit of any other procedure. The book was published in 1977.

Unfinished Tales

Three years later, another volume, *Unfinished Tales*, appeared, containing fourteen long texts, in various stages of incompleteness, on a range of subjects across the legendarium. It included texts of the long versions of two of the three Great Tales, *Tuor and His Coming to Gondolin* (originally meant to be a full retelling of the fall of the city, the first since 1917) and substantial fragments of the *Tale of the Children of Húrin*. A complete text of the latter appeared in April 2007.

History of Middle Earth

Christopher Tolkien now began the enormous task of preparing and publishing the component texts that underlay the 1977 *Silmarillion*. The result, embracing also drafts of *The Lord of the Rings* and various miscellaneous works (such as the unfinished 'time travel' novels, *The Lost Road* and *The Notion Club Papers*), was published in twelve volumes between 1983 and 1996, under the overarching title of *The History of Middle Earth*. This, taken together with his earlier work on *The Silmarillion* and *Unfinished Tales*, is a very considerable work of textual scholarship. Tolkien and his readers have been fortunate in his literary executor, who combines an exhaustive knowledge of the material, expertise in his father's academic interests, and training in the delicate and rigorous art of editing texts. It has been said that we have one man's genius as interpreted over two lifetimes.

Academic texts

The Monsters and the Critics collects seven 'essays' by Tolkien (in fact, all but one were originally public lectures) on academic subjects. It includes the famous *Beowulf* lecture, his lecture on fairy stories, and two texts ('English and Welsh' and 'A Secret Vice'), giving extensive reflexion on Tolkien's own linguistic taste, and on his 'private languages'. None of the pieces is overly technical, indeed Tolkien's written style (as opposed to his spoken delivery, which was reportedly terrible) is beguiling. For anyone interested in the intellectual sources of Tolkien's fiction, or indeed in the language and literature of the old North, this is the best place to start.

His translation of three Middle English poems (*Sir Gawain and the Green Knight*, *Pearl*, and *Sir Orfeo*) into modern English verse was published in 1975. Lecture series on two Old English texts (*Exodus* and *Finn and Hengest*) have also appeared, as have the Völsung and Gudrún poems from the early 1930s (*Sigurd and Gudrún*, May 2009). Tolkien made two translations of *Beowulf*, a complete one in prose, and a partial one (six hundred lines) in alliterative verse; a projected edition of them seems to have stalled.

Linguistic writings

In the early 1990s, Christopher Tolkien entrusted the great bulk of his father's purely linguistic manuscripts (those dealing, that is, with his invented languages) to a group of

American scholars. The materials amount to roughly three thousand pages. Some of the material has been published, in the journals *Vinyar Tengwar* and *Parma Eldalamberon*.

Still unpublished

A volume of Tolkien's *Letters* appeared in 1981; it is a fascinating book, containing three hundred and fifty letters; many of them are abridged, however, and they represent only a fraction of the surviving letters (which number at least fifteen hundred, with more still coming to light). This is the only part of Tolkien's extensive private papers ever to be published. The rest are not available for general consultation, and there are no immediate plans for their publication.

Tolkien the Catholic

There are two aspects under which to consider Tolkien as a Catholic.

First, there is the witness of his life. He was throughout his life a faithful Mass-goer, and a man who took prayer seriously. He counselled one of his sons to learn prayers of praise by heart: he recommended, what he himself found helpful, the Glory Be, the *Gloria*, Psalms 112 and 116, the *Magnificat*, the Litany of Loreto, and the prayer *Sub tuum praesidium*. Tolkien himself usually said his prayers in Latin, although this was simple habit rather than any sense of obligation.[26] He also suggested learning the Canon of the Mass by heart, so that it could be recited privately if circumstances prevented one getting to Mass.[27] If this seems a daunting regimen, we should remember that as a boy he had served Fr Francis Morgan's Mass daily, and was doubtless saturated with the rhythms of the Latin liturgy.

He had a great devotion to the Blessed Sacrament, although reluctance to make his confession (which he had been brought up to think an essential preliminary) sometimes meant he abstained from communion for a time.

Religion, then, consisted for him of the sacraments and private prayer; he did not, like CS Lewis, feel under a duty to engage in public evangelism or intellectual justification of belief. He was not wholly uninvolved in the wider life of the Church, however; in 1944 he was a founder member, and Vice-President, of the Oxford Circle of the Catenians, an association of Catholic professional men. On the whole, though, organised religion (apart from Sunday Mass) did not play an obviously great part in Tolkien's religious life; but this was not unusual amongst Catholics of his time.

He was in favour of ecumenical initiatives with other Christian bodies, but the liturgical changes of the mid-late 1960s were not to his taste. One of his grandsons remembers him at Mass determinedly making the responses in Latin at an English-language Mass; but although the aesthetic of the reformed Rite was not his, and he thought the English translation deplorable, he made no fuss about the validity of the Rite. He remained an obedient son of the Church: "There is nowhere else to go! ...there is nothing to do but to pray…and meanwhile to exercise the virtue of loyalty, which indeed only becomes a virtue when one is under pressure to desert it."[28]

The second aspect of Tolkien's Catholicism is its presence in his writings. There is a sense in which this presence is so structural, so basic to his imagination, that analysis of it risks (as he said of the author of *Beowulf*) pushing over the tower to see where he got his building material.

Tolkien insisted to his friend, the convert and Jesuit Robert Murray, that *The Lord of the Rings* was "a fundamentally religious and Catholic work."[29] It is interesting to note some superficial connections,[30] but too much should not be made of them. Many were entirely adventitious developments, not essential elements of the story; easy parallels between his story and Christianity (Frodo as a 'type' of Christ, for example) were things Tolkien himself always resisted. Insofar as they are valid, it is only because the moral pattern of Christianity (with regard, say, to suffering and its value) is a universally applicable one and thus holds for his characters as much as for anyone else. The story, he strongly insisted, is just that: a story, not an allegory of the Christian life.

What makes Tolkien a specifically Christian writer, and his books specifically Christian books, is his absolute conviction of the power and validity, under God, of our capacity to tell stories - and in particular *fantasy* stories.

The short story *Leaf by Niggle* is illuminating here. Niggle is a painter, working on a great canvas of a Tree, which is perpetually ramifying and taking over more of his life. He is also constantly interrupted; the last of these interruptions prevents him finishing the picture before he dies. After passage through Purgatory, and reconciliation with his bothersome neighbour, he finds his Tree, finished and alive, set in a landscape on the approaches to the Mountains, which are God's country, heaven. This puts in fictional form an insight Tolkien expressed forcibly to CS Lewis, and later put into his poem *Mythopoeia*: that our stories, particularly as they approach that high style we call 'myth,' necessarily and inevitably express something of God's truth, precisely because this is what human beings do. He does not mean that stories must be allegories, in which characters and events 'stand for' particular moral or spiritual truths (in fact, he disliked this type of story); rather, any well-told tale will convey some elements of God's truth not normally or otherwise expressible. In his lecture 'On Fairy Stories', Tolkien elaborated his theory, which he called 'sub-creation': art and story exist because human beings, as images of God the Creator, are by nature makers, and creators of 'secondary worlds'. God may even choose, *Leaf by Niggle* suggests, to give a measure of primary reality (the 'Secret Fire') to these products of our secondary art.

As was mentioned earlier, Tolkien's constant theme was "death: inevitable death." The message of *Leaf by Niggle*, inasmuch as it can be reduced to a single item, is that death is not the end of sub-creation, but a way to the fulfilment of it, to the achieving of what we had long ago despaired of ever finishing, let alone of bringing to the very perfection that, in vision, had inspired us: to its incorporation into the loving plan of God. This is one of Tolkien's approaches to the problem; the other is through the elves: they are above all makers, of song, story, works of hand and mind, freed from the limits imposed by a human life-span and gifted with skill beyond human measure. They are arch-subcreators who are yet bounded by the world in a way men are not.

The Silmarils are the great embodiment of elvish art; but they are also the cause of their maker's ruin, and that of his whole people, who are caught by selfish love of what has been made, rather than joy in the making and giving. An image of God-given beauty can, too easily, become an idol; the elven dilemma is our own writ large.

There is, then, at the heart of Tolkien's work a conviction that what we say, and in particular the tales we tell, express as well as anything else we do the image we bear of the Creator God, the gift granted our first parents, not wholly lost by them in the Fall, and now redeemed - both rescued from debility and made new and greater - by the Incarnation. Even death, which Tolkien once named as his greatest theme, is now not wholly a defeat, but a means despite itself of greater victory, beyond hope or expectation.

He also gives a profound, if unfashionable, reflection on the nature of evil, and the temporary and provisional nature of our victories over it in this life, whether small and private victories over vice, or great national triumphs over a tyrant or oppressor. In one sense, the Northern theory of courage was true: defeat, in this world, was inevitable, and all our hopes and schemes and efforts would fail. But this was still the proper side to fight on, and courage in its service was the only proper attitude. The Christian revelation does not abolish 'Northern courage'; rather it fulfils and redeems it, because it adds that, beyond the end of all things in defeat and fire, there is a new life, and a redeemed world, healed from its hurts and new-made according to its Creator's mind, only this time further enriched and made beautiful by the works of his children. This is the whole burden, in one sense, of *The Silmarillion*, from its creation story to its prophecy of the End. Tolkien's elves are bound to the circles of the world, and endure whilst it does, tending and making as they live, enfolded in and in some way giving voice to its joys and sorrows; but man's fate lies beyond the world, in the good counsels of the One.

Further Reading

The first place to start is with Tolkien's own writings.

The best source for his life remains Humphrey Carpenter's authorised biography; Carpenter is the only writer ever to have had access to Tolkien's private papers, and this alone gives his book enduring value, although obviously it does not cover most of the posthumously published work in full. It is usefully supplemented by Carpenter's later book *The Inklings* (Allen and Unwin, 1978), which is especially good on CS Lewis. More recently, John Garth's *Tolkien and the Great War* (HarperCollins, 2003) gives invaluable detail on Tolkien's early life. Anyone seeking additional detail should consult the magisterial and very comprehensive *JRR Tolkien: A Companion and Guide* by Christina Scull and Wayne Hammond (two volumes, HarperCollins, 2006).

The best work on Tolkien's academic background and its fundamental importance to his writing is Tom Shippey's *The Road to Middle Earth* (HarperCollins, third edition, 2003), supplemented by his later collection, *Roots and Branches* (Zurich and Berne, Switzerland, Walking Tree Publishers,

2007). Also useful are *The Ring of Words: Tolkien and the Oxford English Dictionary* by three of the *OED's* current editors (Oxford, OUP, 2006), and *Tolkien the Medievalist* (ed. Jane Chance, New York, Routledge, 2003). For literary criticism of Tolkien, the best place to start is again with Shippey, *Tolkien: Author of the Century* (HarperCollins, 2000). For the philosophical and theological undercurrents in Tolkien, see Stratford Caldecott's *The Power of the Ring* (New York, Crossroad, 2012, which incorporates his earlier book *Secret Fire*), and Peter Kreeft's *The Philosophy of Tolkien* (Ignatius Press, 2005).

There are hundreds of other books - big and small, good and bad - on Tolkien and his writings; some of them are listed in the works named above.

There are also very many websites, ranging from guides to Tolkien's Oxford to comprehensive encyclopedias of everything Tolkien-related. Any search engine will readily provide.

Endnotes

[1] *The Notion Club Papers*, in *Sauron Defeated* (volume 9 of *The History of Middle Earth*, 12 vols, ed. Christopher Tolkien (London, George Allen & Unwin/HarperCollins, 1983-1996): henceforth *HME*) p.233.

[2] The family told stories of how their ancestors were originally Saxon nobility, given the soubriquet *tollkühn* or 'foolhardy' after heroism at the 1529 siege of Vienna, and driven to England by one invasion or other. Many middle-class families preserve similar aristocratic origin stories, which may contain smaller or larger elements of truth. Certainly there are Tolkiehns and Tolkiens in Lower Saxony and Hamburg today.

[3] Her sister had also just returned from South Africa with two small boys; her husband, like Arthur Tolkien, stayed behind. Unlike Arthur, he survived to make the journey, and on his arrival forbade his wife to enter a Catholic church again. She instead took up with spiritualism.

[4] Humphrey Carpenter, *J.R.R. Tolkien: A Biography* (London, George Allen & Unwin, 1977), p.31.

[5] *The Letters of J.R.R. Tolkien*, edd. Humphrey Carpenter and Christopher Tolkien (London, George Allen & Unwin, 1980; often reprinted; henceforth *Letters*), p. 395, (to Michael Tolkien, 1967/1968).

[6] Tolkien used this term in a number of letters written between 1951 and 1955; historically, it means a collection of saints' lives, but has become accepted shorthand amongst writers on Tolkien, so I have adopted it for convenience.

[7] Grimm, collector of fairytales, was a mighty philologist, one of whose many achievements was the great *Deutsche Mythologie*, built from hints and words as much as from surviving legends.

[8] Gilson had joined the Suffolk Regiment, Wiseman the Navy, where his mathematics were put to use range-finding on the dreadnought HMS Superb. He saw action at Jutland at the end of May.

[9] *Letters* p. 46 (to Michael Tolkien, 6th October 1940).

[10] Quoted in Carpenter, *The Inklings*, pp. 22 – 23.

[11] *Letters*, p. 362 (to Dick Plotz, 12th September 1965).

[12] Carpenter, *Biography*, p. 148 and *Inklings*, p. 32.

[13] *Letters*, p. 416. Fr Francis left Tolkien and his brother £1,000 each in his will.

[14] *Letters*, p. 346 (to Christopher Bretherton, 16th July 1964). See also the account in *HME* Vol. 3 pp. 364-367.

[15] He also wrote a new fifth chapter for *The Hobbit*, to make it better fit with the later story; he sent it speculatively to Unwin on 21st September 1947, and was surprised to find it printed, without further ado, in the next edition of *The Hobbit*.

[16] It was finally published in 1954, and runs to fully seven hundred pages. When the series had originally been mooted in 1935, Tolkien had been asked to write a volume on Old English literature, but had refused owing to lack of time.

[17] For details, see Carpenter, *The Inklings*, pp. 229-230.

[18] *Letters*, p. 172.

[19] Joy's cancer eventually returned, and she died in July 1960. The following year, Lewis published, anonymously, *A Grief Observed*, one of the most honest accounts of bereavement ever written.

[20] Despite their (to him inexplicable) personal estrangement, Lewis still promoted Tolkien's work. In 1961, he nominated Tolkien for the Nobel Prize for Literature; Tolkien was rejected, on the grounds that he did not tell stories well enough. The Prize that year went, instead, to a Bosnian folklorist.

[21] 26th Nov 1963; *Letters*, p. 341.

[22] 11th November 1964; *Letters*, p. 352.

[23] Kilby, *Tolkien and the Silmarillion* (Lion, 1977), p. 20.

[24] *Letters*, p. 420 (to Christopher Tolkien, 11th July 1972).

[25] *Letters*, p. 431 (to Lord Halsbury, 4th August 1973).

[26] He composed Quenya versions of five prayers - the Our Father, Hail Mary, Glory Be, *Sub tuum praesidium* and the Litany of Loreto - but there is no suggestion he used these devotionally.

[27] To Christopher Tolkien, 8th January 1944; *Letters* p. 66.

[28] *Letters*, p. 393 (to Michael Tolkien, 1967/68).

[29] 2nd December 1953; *Letters*, p. 172. Murray's grandfather was the great Sir James Murray, founder of the *OED*.

[30] Notably, the destruction of the Ring, and the power of Sauron, on 25th March, a date on which thereafter "the New Year will always now begin"; it is also, of course, the feast of the Annunciation, which marks the coming of Christ into the womb of Mary, and thus the beginning of defeat of death and sin, and was until the eighteenth century the start of the calendar year. We could also instance the Elvish invocations of Elbereth (Varda) as analogous to Marian devotion.

Understanding the New Age Movement

Stratford Caldecott

The New Age Movement is regarded by many Christians as a
growing threat to traditional beliefs and practices.
Why are so many people attracted to astrology, reincarnation and
magic, to spiritualism and goddess-worship, to new cults and old
heresies? This clear and thoroughly researched text explores the
meaning and direction of the New Age Movement in relation to
Catholic teaching, and asks how Catholics can best respond
to the challenge it represents.

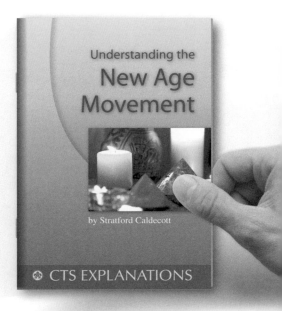

LUMEN
The Catholic Gift to Civilisation

Fr Andrew Pinsent, Fr Marcus Holden

In a recent debate, broadcast worldwide by the BBC, over 87% of the audience rejected the motion that the Catholic Church is a force for good in the world. To set the record straight, this booklet summarises the extraordinary fruitfulness of the faith, noting that our university system, art, music, legal tradition, charity and even much of our science arises from Catholic civilisation and Catholic minds.

Ev 6   ISBN 978 1 86082 725 9

A world of Catholic reading at your fingertips...

Catholic Faith, Life & Truth for all

www.cts-online.org.uk

CTS CATHOLIC COMPASS

ctscatholiccompass.org

twitter: @CTSpublishers

facebook.com/CTSpublishers

Catholic Truth Society, Publishers to the Holy See.